T0132390

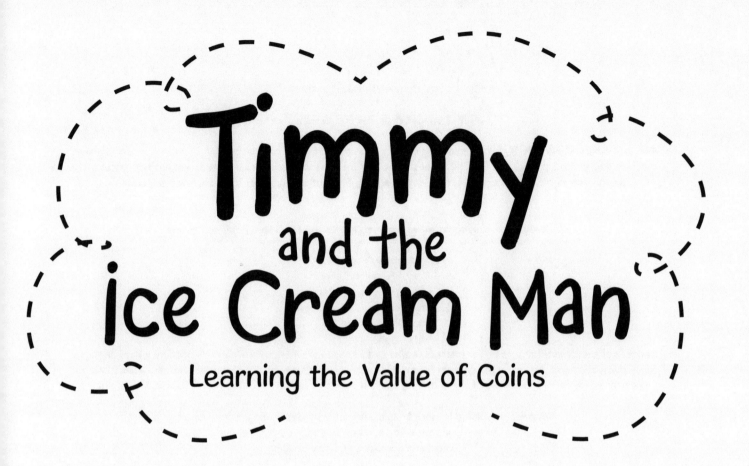

Timmy
and the
Ice Cream Man

Learning the Value of Coins

GAIL LOCKHART

Archway Publishing books may be ordered through booksellers or by contacting:

Archway Publishing
1663 Liberty Drive
Bloomington, IN 47403
www.archwaypublishing.com
1 (888) 242-5904

ISBN: 978-1-4808-7451-0 (sc)
ISBN: 978-1-4808-7450-3 (e)

Print information available on the last page.

Archway Publishing rev. date: 02/06/2019

This book is dedicated to my Grandsons,

Tavian and Teagan,

who inspired me to write it.

"Timmy come here for a minute," said grandma
as he was walking by her bedroom.

"Okay Grandma" replied Timmy.

"Timmy, I remember promising you money for an ice cream because you helped me do the dishes last night."

"Here is some change I have, but I don't know if it is enough. Your mother knows how much the ice cream man charges for his ice cream so go ask her if it is enough," said grandma.

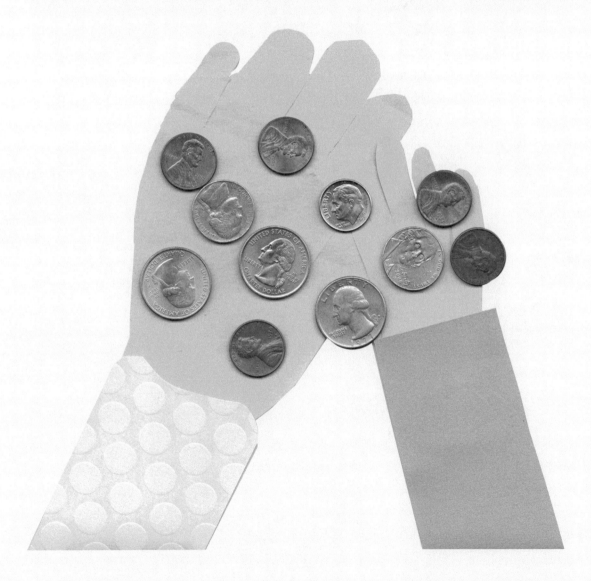

"Mom, Grandma gave me some money to buy an ice cream, but she is not sure if she gave me enough. Did she?" asked Timmy.

"I don't know Timmy, put the coins on the table and let us find out," replied mom

Timmy, the ice cream man charges $1.00 for his ice cream so let's see if Grandma gave you enough money.

"Timmy, can you tell me how much money is there?" asked mom.

"No," replied Timmy.

"Would you like to learn?" asked mom.

"Yes, please mom," replied Timmy.

"Timmy let us start with the pennies. The pennies are the copper colored coins. The others are all silver colored. Can you count how many pennies you have?" asked mom.

"I have 5 pennies Mom," said Timmy. "That is correct Timmy," replied mom. "Five pennies are equal to one nickel."

"Can you show me which coin is a nickel?" asked mom

"It is this one Mom. I remember because Dad
gave me a nickel once," said Timmy.

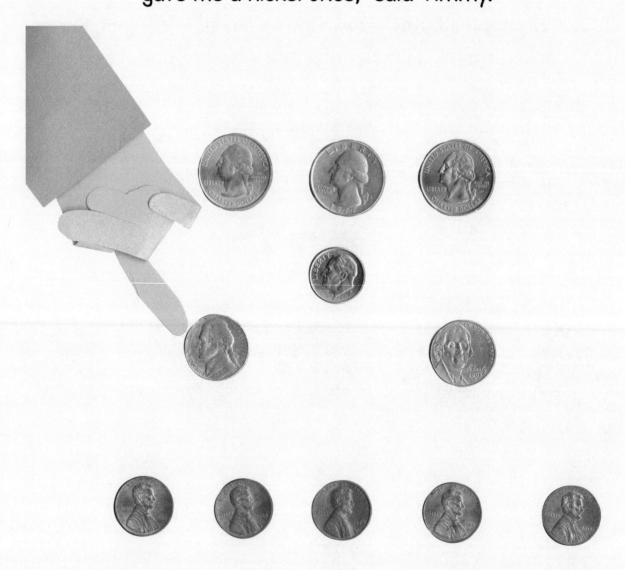

"That's good," said mom. "Two nickels are equal to one dime. What else is here that equals a dime?" asked mom.

Timmy thought about that for a minute and excitedly replied "One nickel and five pennies equals a dime!"

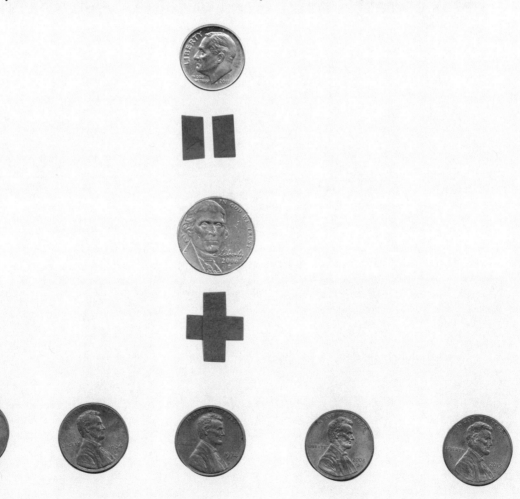

"So, Timmy what is another way to make a dime?"

"Mom so if a nickel and five pennies equal a dime
then the dime is the same as ten pennies."

"That is correct Timmy. Good thinking!" answered mom

"Timmy what coin is next?" asked mom.

"The big coin," answered Timmy.

"Timmy those big coins are quarters. How many quarters do we have?" asked mom.

"We have three quarters mom," replied Timmy.

"Timmy each quarter is equal to 1 dime, 2 nickels, and 5 pennies."
Said mom. How many pennies is a quarter worth?" asked mom.

After thinking about it, Timmy said "Mom
a quarter is worth 25 pennies."

"That is correct," replied mom.

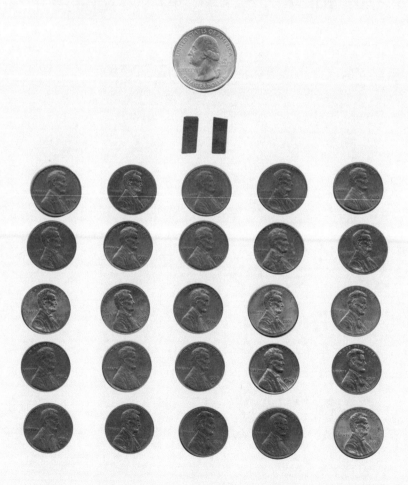

"How much did I say the ice cream man charged for his ice cream?" asked mom.

"$1.00 dollar" said Timmy

Timmy thought about this for about 1 minute, jumped up from his chair excitedly and said," Mom, quarters are 25 cents each and I have three of them, which equals 75 cents. If I add one dime, I have 85 cents. I add two nickels I have 95 cents plus 5 pennies equal one dollar, which is enough for an ice cream!

"Timmy, I hear the ice cream truck coming down the street" said mom. Let's go get your ice cream!

Printed in the United States
By Bookmasters